W9-ADY-000

INDUSTRIAL MINERALS

How They Are Found and Used

Robert L. Bates

— an Earth Resources book —

ENSLOW PUBLISHERS, INC.

Bloy St. & Ramsey Ave.	P.O. Box 38
Box 777	Aldershot
Hillside, N.J. 07205	Hants GU12 6BP
U.S.A.	U.K.

Library of Congress Cataloging-in-Publication Data

Bates, Robert Latimer, 1912-
  Industrial minerals.

  (An Earth resources book)
  Bibliography: p.
  Includes index.
  Summary: Describes mineral resources used in such
industries as agriculture, printing, and glassmaking,
and explains the discovery, mining, and exploitation
of deposits.
  1. Mines and mineral resources--Juvenile literature.
[1. Mines and mineral resources]   I. Title. II. Series.
TN148.B37   1988   553.6   87-36537
ISBN 0-89490-174-5

Printed in the United States of America

10 9 8 7 6 5 4 3 2

ILLUSTRATION CREDITS:
Courtesy of: Cargill, Inc., pp. 1, 2; English China Clays Group, p. 10; Florida Phosphate Council, pp. 12, 13; Freeport Sulfur Company, p. 16; Georgia Kaolin Company, pp. 8, 9, 11; GE Specialty Materials Department, p. 21; Gouverneur Talc Company, p. 24; Saskatchewan Government Photos, pp. 3, 4; Stauffer Chemical Company of Wyoming, p. 5; U.S. Geological Survey, pp. 18, 19, 23, 27.

Contents

Preface

Four big groups of earth materials support our complex modern society. Ore deposits give us iron, copper, aluminum, and the other metals. Mineral fuels power our cars, heat our homes, and run our factories. Stone products enable us to build with concrete, brick, and glass. And a broad assortment of other earth materials go into paper, paint, plastics, chemicals, filters, films, fertilizers, and a host of other products. These industrial minerals are the subject of this book.

As you might expect, these essential minerals are found in a wide variety of deposits in the earth's crust. So we'll be talking about quite an array of rocks and minerals and their geologic settings. These will be explained as we go along.

Robert L. Bates

1

Salts of the Earth

A single geological process has produced deposits of several valuable earth materials. That process is evaporation. At various times in the geologic past, lakes or shallow seas became enriched in certain elements, and then, under a torrid sun, gradually dried up, leaving behind their mineral content as beds of crystalline salts. These evaporites, as they are called, include salt, sylvite, trona, and borax.

Salt

Aside from water, only one substance in the earth's crust that we use directly is absolutely essential to our existence. We use it every time we reach for the salt shaker. Because salt is essential to life, it has been sought and used since the dawn of history. From the salt mines of northern India to the shores of the Dead Sea, ancient lands were crisscrossed with trails made by salt caravans. The Bible says, "Can that which is unsavory be eaten without salt?" Caesar's soldiers received a part of their pay (their "salarium," or salary) in the form of salt. Since salt was a universal necessity and its supply could be controlled, it was an ideal substance for taxation—a fact that received rulers' attention from the earliest times. Smuggling, hijacking, and black-marketeering probably have ancient origins in people's desire to escape a burdensome tax on salt.

Salt occurs as a white crystalline rock, consisting of just one mineral, halite (sodium chloride, NaCl). Today, only a small part of the salt produced is used to preserve or flavor food. Salt is an industrial chemical: its sodium is used in many processes and products, and its chlorine in many others. Salt keeps our roads free of ice in the winter. It is also used in water softening, textile manufacture, and many other applications.

In Late Silurian time (about 410 million years ago), thick beds of salt accumulated by evaporation in a marine basin that extended from what is now western New York into Ohio, Michigan, and Ontario. Other great salt basins existed in the

Salt from underground. The two arms, in left corner and foreground, rotate in a scooping motion, gathering salt onto the belt at center which moves it to a conveyor.

Middle Devonian (about 375 million years ago) in the North Dakota-Montana-Saskatchewan region; in Late Permian time (about 230 million years ago) from Kansas southwest into Texas and New Mexico; and in the Jurassic period (about 150 million years ago) beneath what is now the Gulf Coastal Plain of Texas and Louisiana. Other basins occur on other continents.

Rock salt is easily dissolved in rain water, so deposits at the earth's surface are found only in arid regions. At Bonneville Salt Flats in Utah, for example, salt was deposited when Lake Bonneville, a big lake of the Ice Age, evaporated as the climate warmed and rainfall decreased. (Great Salt Lake is all that's left of Lake Bonneville.) Thin surface deposits of salt are locally mined, but the big deposits formed in ancient seas are always underground, where overlying rocks have preserved them from solution. In these deposits, mining

More than 30,000 tons of salt can be stored in this underground chamber at a Gulf Coast mine. Conveyors hoist the salt nearly 1,600 feet (488 meters) to the surface.

is generally done by the room-and-pillar method, in which about half the salt is removed, the remainder being left in pillars to support the mine roof. For example, salt comes from such a mine beneath the city of Cleveland, at a depth of 1,770 feet (540 meters); the mine extends out under Lake Erie. Salt may also be obtained by solution mining. Wells are drilled into the salt beds, and water is pumped down to dissolve the salt before returning to the surface. The "artificial brine" that results may be evaporated to yield solid salt, or introduced directly into processes of chemical manufacture. About 10 percent of our salt is obtained by evaporating sea water, which contains 3.5 percent of salt, in shallow ponds that are allowed to evaporate so that the salt can then be harvested.

Considering the immense quantities of salt available, both in the rocks and in the ocean, it is clear that there will be no shortage of this essential mineral for an infinite time to come.

Sylvite

Sylvite is a white, colorless, or flesh-pink mineral with the simple composition KCl—potassium chloride. (The K stands for "kalium," Latin for potassium.) Sylvite occurs intergrown with another simple chloride, halite or common salt (NaCl). Salt-sylvite beds are the relics of ancient seas that evaporated to almost complete dryness. Both minerals dissolve readily in near-surface waters, so deposits are found only below a cover of younger rocks and must be mined underground.

Nearly all the production of sylvite, plus that of a few less important potassium minerals, is used in fertilizer. If you've been involved in home gardening, you have encountered sylvite in packaged "NPK" fertilizer. This is a blend of compounds containing nitrogen, phosphorus, and potassium. The sylvite content may give the material a pinkish color.

The name potassium is a Latinized form of an ancient workaday term, potash. For centuries, water was filtered, or leached, through wood ashes and then evaporated in iron pots. The resulting "pot ash" was used in dyeing and tanning, and in making soap, matches, and other household needs. It was also known to be a useful plant food. "Potash" is now a general term, used in commerce, to apply to a variety of potassium minerals and compounds.

Up to the time of the Civil War, our needs for potassium fertilizer were met chiefly by the leaching of wood ashes. Then big deposits of sylvite-bearing rocks were found in Germany, and the United States shortly became dependent on this source. But it was obvious that we needed our own sources. This need led to development of deposits in southeastern New Mexico, where for years oil-company geologists had been reporting potassium-bearing minerals in well cuttings and cores from rocks of Late Permian age (235 million years old). By 1931, commercial mining was under way from

A continuous-mining machine in a potash deposit in Saskatchewan, Canada. Bits at left rotate as the machine moves forward; broken rock emerges at the back.

beneath the desert plains east of Carlsbad, New Mexico. These deposits, rich in svlvite, soon made the United States self-sufficient, and, in fact, an exporter of potash. Then, in the 1950s, immense deposits were discovered in Middle Devonian rocks (375 million years old) beneath the plains of Saskatchewan in western Canada. Although the Carlsbad district is still productive, the focus of the industry has shifted to the larger and richer deposits in Canada.

Flat-lying beds of salt-plus-sylvite are relatively easy to cut, and some of them are mined by continuous-mining machines that bore big passages through the deposits. Salt and sylvite are separated in a mill; the resulting product is nearly pure potassium chloride. It is usable by plants to promote root growth and resist disease. The refined product is shipped by rail in covered hopper cars, and is handled at special weatherproof storage facilities in farming centers.

Maintenance room 3,145 feet (959 meters) below the surface in a Saskatchewan potash mine. Walls show grooves left by continuous-mining machines. Entrance to mining area is at lower left. Mining crews travel on personnel carriers like the one at lower right.

Trona

Trona (a name of Arabic origin) is a light-colored crystalline mineral, a hydrous sodium carbonate, $Na_3H(CO_3)_2 \cdot 2H_2O$. Long known as one of the minerals on the surface of dried-up salt lakes, trona had never been found in quantity. Then, early in 1938, wildcatters drilling for oil on the plains of southwestern Wyoming struck an unexpected kind of "pay." Between the depths of 1,590 and 1,600 feet (485 and 488 meters), the drill penetrated a solid layer of trona. Though the well turned out to be a dry hole, it made a discovery that completely changed one segment of this country's chemical industry.

Sodium carbonate, Na_2CO_3, is known commercially as *soda ash*. It is one of the three substances from which glass is made. It is also used in making paper, detergents, water softeners, and many other products, including (naturally enough) washing soda and baking soda. At the time of the trona discovery, and for 100 years before that, soda ash had been manufactured, in a process devised by two Belgian brothers, Ernst and Alfred Solvay. In this process, a salt brine is saturated with carbon dioxide from a lime kiln, and a sodium-bicarbonate slurry is formed. The sodium bicarbonate is then filtered from the liquid.

The Wyoming discovery of trona changed the picture dramatically. In 1938, seventeen Solvay-process plants were producing soda ash in this country; by 1969 the number had dropped to ten; today there are none. The natural material has taken over. The product is even being exported to Europe, to the consternation of the long-established Solvay industry there.

In the field of industrial minerals there are numerous examples of manufactured products that have taken markets away from naturally occurring minerals. The soda-ash picture is a notable development in the opposite direction.

Exploratory drilling that followed the discovery showed that enormous amounts of trona are present in the subsurface of southwestern Wyoming. Commercial production started in 1946. By 1980, four companies were mining trona, at depths ranging from 800 to 1,500 feet (235 to 457 meters). The mineral is refined in large plants, by a series of chemical processes, to produce pure sodium carbonate. The district is crossed by the Union Pacific Railroad, so that transportation is assured.

The beds of trona accumulated in a lake, which occupied a broad shallow depression, the Green River Basin, in Eocene time (about 50 million years ago). Some 1200 square

In this trona mine in Wyoming, the roof is stabilized by bolting. The operator directs a machine that drills a hole upward. He will then insert a rod with an expander at the upper end and a plate at the lower. Turning the bolt fastens the roof securely to overlying strata. Plates in the roof mark earlier bolts.

miles (3109 square kilometers) are underlain by beds of trona; there are layers of volcanic ash and other sediments as well. Some of the trona is intergrown with halite (common salt), so these minerals are probably products of evaporation as the lake waters shrank during dry spells.

The Green River Basin is one of about ten similar basins in the Rocky Mountain region, but only one other basin contains sodium salts, and these in far smaller amounts. Why did 5,000 million tons of sodium carbonate accumulate in the Green River Basin but little or none in the others? The answer seems to lie in volcanic action. Some sodium was contributed by volcanic ash that fell into the lake; more would have come via streams that drained the adjacent ash-blanketed lands. And then there were hot springs; some of these, as at Soda Springs, Idaho, are still active in the region. So the trona apparently originated in volcanic processes from within the Earth.

Borax

Borax is a clear to translucent mineral that occurs in crystalline clusters. It is a sodium borate, with an unusually large amount—10 molecules—of water: $Na_2B_4O_7 \cdot 10H_2O$. Unlike trona, which is a latecomer on the commercial scene, borax has been used for centuries. In Asia Minor and the Far East, it was used in welding and coating precious metals, and in glazing fine chinaware. (The word *borax* comes from an Arabic word, "bouracq.") Marco Polo brought borax crystals to Europe in the thirteenth century. Deposits were later discovered in Italy and Turkey. United States production began in 1864; by 1887, this country was the world's chief supplier of borax, from dry-lake deposits in Nevada and Death Valley, California. These deposits were many miles from a railroad, and the borax was moved across the desert to the railhead in big wagons pulled by mules. For years, "20-mule-team borax" was one of the best known trade names in the country.

It was not until 1925 that our biggest deposit was found. Drilling revealed massive beds of borax at shallow depth at a place in the Mojave Desert now known as Boron. Fortunately, it was right on the Santa Fe Railroad. A large open pit today supplies more than half the world's demand for borax. Much of the remainder comes from mines in Turkey.

Borax is valuable in glassmaking because it lowers the temperature at which the raw materials will melt and thus reduces the amount of energy required. It also makes glass resistant to heat: half of the United States production goes into ovenware like Pyrex, and into other special grades of glass. A relatively new use is the flameproofing of a fluffy thermal insulation made from shredded newspaper. Borax is a raw material of boric acid and of soaps and detergents.

The deposit at Boron, California, accumulated in a desert lake in Pliocene time, somewhat more than 2 million years ago. It was a small lake, with an area only a tiny fraction of the trona lake in Wyoming. Borax occurs in beds as much as 35 feet (10.7 meters) thick. These beds are enclosed in gray shale, which is impervious and has protected the borax from solution in underground water. The borax is mined in an open pit, separated from the shale and refined in a nearby plant, and shipped by rail.

This deposit is apparently the only one of its kind in North America. Its origin is almost certainly connected with volcanic activity. Lava flows are close by; evidently boron-rich hot waters were poured out with the lava. Accumulating in the adjacent desert basin from time to time, these waters evaporated and borax was precipitated. Mud that was washed into the basin covered and protected the soluble salts. Although the whole deposit occupies less than one square mile, it is one of the world's major concentrations of a valuable industrial mineral.

2

High-Class Clays

Ordinary clay, as you probably know, is formed into bricks, tiles, and similar everyday products. It is one of the commonest of earth materials. But ordinary clay has several aristocratic cousins, with special properties and uses. These include bentonite, china clay, and paper clay.

Bentonite

On May 18, 1980, Mount St. Helens, a volcano in Washington state, erupted with a violent blast that sent volcanic ash 63,000 feet (19,202 meters) into the air. As it settled, the ash blanketed hundreds of square miles. This eruption, although a catastrophe by local standards, was mild compared to some that have happened in the geologic past. Old beds of volcanic ash are known that are several feet thick instead of a few inches. Some of them cover thousands of square miles.

You might think that "volcanic ash" is a product of burning, but it isn't; it is just finely shattered rock material. It is not very stable in terms of geologic time. Eventually rainfall and underground water alter the ash to a variety of clay, called bentonite. This material takes its name from Fort Benton, an old-time army outpost in Montana. Much bentonite comes from Wyoming, South Dakota, and Montana, where it occurs in flat-lying beds near the surface. These are altered ash beds of Cretaceous age (about 80 million years old). The bentonite is dug from open pits, dried, and ground to fine powder. No other processing is necessary.

What is this bentonite good for? Among other things, it has the property of absorbing large quantities of water, swelling greatly as it does so. Once dispersed in water, the clay stays in suspension indefinitely; in other words, it forms a "colloidal gel," from which the solid particles will not settle out. This property is utilized in drilling wells for oil and gas. A steel bit at the bottom of a length of steel pipe is rotated, just like a carpenter's bit cutting into wood. As the bit bores its way downward through the rocks, it is obviously necessary

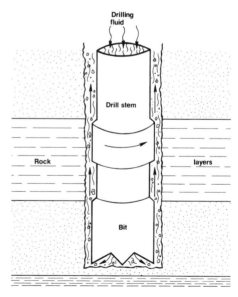

Circulating fluid makes possible deep drilling by the rotary method. It lubricates the bit and lifts the rock chips off the bottom of the hole. Bentonite and barite are common in drilling fluids.

16

to remove the ground-up rock from the bottom of the hole. Also, the bit must be lubricated and cooled. To meet these needs, while drilling proceeds a fluid is pumped from the surface down the inside of the drill pipe, through holes in the bit, and back up to the surface between the pipe and the walls of the hole. It carries the rock chips to a pit on the surface, where they are removed before the fluid is recirculated.

In the early days of the oil industry, drilling fluid was simply mud—water mixed with whatever clayey material happened to be handy. But as wells became deeper, and drilling was better developed, a more uniform and efficient fluid was

Bentonite in action: drilling fluid at an oil well being drilled in Nigeria.

needed. Bentonite in water proved to be the answer. This drilling fluid is slippery and lubricates the bit. The dispersed clay not only helps lift the ground-up rock from the bottom of the hole, but it also plasters the walls of the hole, preventing water from entering and making it easy to rotate the drill pipe. Thus two essential earth products—oil and gas—are produced with the help of a third—bentonite.

Bentonite has other uses. It forms a binder in holding foundry sands together to receive molten metal. It is combined with finely ground iron ore, to "pelletize" the ore and make it easy to ship and handle. A variety of bentonite has the property of absorbing such substances as oil, grease, and animal wastes. If your household includes a cat, the chances are that the material with which you periodically line its litter box is crumbly, absorbent bentonite.

China clay

People have been making earthenware containers from clay since prehistoric times. Nevertheless, this activity was a minor and rather backward industry as recently as the mid-1700s. An English potter named Josiah Wedgwood, who went into business in 1759, changed the picture. Instead of using low-quality local clays, he started making products of a pure light-colored clay of the type that had been used in China. A variety of this clay that was available in England is known as "ball clay," from an early custom of rolling freshly dug clay into balls for shipment. Wedgwood began producing handsome cream-colored table china, which he named Queen's Ware (possibly with an eye to royal favor). He also produced delicate vases, and a dinner service for Catherine the Great of Russia. To this day, Wedgwood china is a premium product.

Other products made from china clay include sanitary ware, wall tile, porcelain, and related ceramics.

About 70 percent of china clay consists of a white mineral

called kaolinite. (We have to take the mineralogist's word for this, as the clay minerals are so extremely fine-grained that they can be identified only by very specialized methods.) Kaolinite is a hydrous aluminum silicate. The remainder of the clay includes other clay minerals, quartz grains, and often a little organic matter.

China clay is plastic and can be molded into forms that it will hold. These forms—bowls, vases, tiles, or whatever—are passed through a kiln, where temperatures reach as much as 1300° C (2372° F). Here the clay partially melts; on cooling, the forms are dense, hard whiteware. Clays are often blended to achieve just the right properties in the product. Ground feldspar, talc, or other minerals may be added to the mix.

Ceramic clays are mined in open pits from sedimentary beds in westernmost Kentucky and Tennessee. The deposits accumulated in Eocene time (about 45 million years ago), when the sea extended far up the Mississippi Valley and the area was along the coast. The clay commonly contains enough organic matter to make it gray or even black, but this carbonaceous material burns off in the kiln. The result is a white or near-white coffee cup, wall tile, or other useful product.

Paper clay

The true aristocrat of clays is a white variety called kaolin. The name comes from the Chinese "kauling," meaning high hill and referring to a place where this unusual clay was found. Kaolin consists almost entirely of the mineral kaolinite. Impurities, mainly quartz, are removed in processing.

About 75 percent of the kaolin produced is used in making high-quality paper. Ordinary paper, like newsprint, is made of ground-up wood fibers, chemically treated to make a thin intermeshed sheet. A much better grade of paper is required for picture magazines and other publications that contain high-resolution color photographs. In making paper of this type, kaolin is introduced in water suspension. The particles become trapped among the wood fibers, giving a closely textured surface that is white and smooth. Paper of the finest quality is then coated with a thin film of extra-fine kaolin.

Besides its brilliant white color, kaolin is extremely fine-grained, soft, chemically inert, and easily dispersed in water. It is also opaque, having what is called "good covering power." It produces a high gloss and a surface that holds ink evenly.

Kaolin is formed in nature by the long-continued decay of

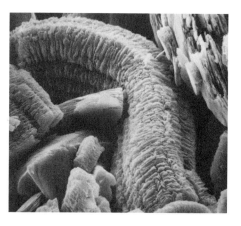

Large crystals of kaolinite (the mineral of kaolin) in stacklike form. These crystals are "delaminated" into separate platelike particles for use in coating paper. Magnified 4,100 times.

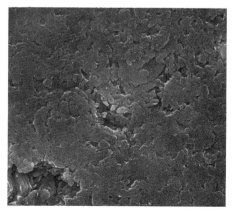

Surface of paper, magnified 5,400 times, after a kaolin coating has been applied.

the mineral feldspar, especially in such rocks as granite. In Cornwall, southwestern England, rocks that were once hard, fresh granite are now a soft crumbly mass of kaolin and quartz grains. High-pressure water jets are used to wash the kaolin into pools at the bottom of deep pits. Here it is separated from the quartz, which is conveyed to waste piles. The kaolin is pumped up to a plant on the surface, where it is washed, filtered, and dried.

The chief United States deposits are of a different kind altogether. They are in sedimentary beds, situated on the coastal plain of Georgia and South Carolina. Streams long

At a pit in Cornwall, England, hydraulic jets wash kaolin out of the decayed granite in which it occurs. The kaolin-water mixture is pumped to a treatment plant on the surface.

ago washed the kaolin from its parent rock—probably a decomposed granite—and brought it to shallow lagoons on the coastal plain. The beds of kaolin are close to the surface and are readily dug by power shovels. The deposits are exceptionally pure.

The Cornwall and the Georgia/South Carolina districts together produce 60 percent of the world's output of kaolin. In a recent year, their combined production was over 10 million tons. The world's demand for high-quality paper, and hence for kaolin, increases all the time.

The next time you pick up a stack of magazines, or a beautifully illustrated book, you may reflect that 30 percent of the weight in your hands is not paper at all, but a high-class clay.

In Georgia, sedimentary beds of kaolin are mined by power equipment. Unit at right mixes the kaolin with water for removal by pipeline.

3

Phosphorus and the King of Chemicals

We must have phosphorus. Together with calcium it makes up our teeth and bones. The word is of Greek origin and means "light-bearer"; it refers to the element's ability to generate light (phosphorescence). "Life-bearer" might be more appropriate. Not only humans and animals require phosphorus: it is also essential as fertilizer for healthy crops.

Phosphorus for use in food-growing comes from rocks in the earth's crust. To make these rocks into useful plant food requires sulfuric acid, a versatile chemical made from another earth material, sulfur. So phosphorus and sulfur may well be discussed together.

Phosphates

Long ago, farmers realized that phosphorus had to be added to croplands. At first, bone meal (ground bones) was applied to the soil. A German chemist named Liebig found that treating bones with sulfuric acid made their phosphorus content more soluble and thus more available to plant roots. But obviously the supply of bones was limited. Phosphorus-bearing rocks were known, but they couldn't be used because they weren't soluble and would not yield their phosphorus. Then, in 1842, an English farmer named John Lawes found that the phosphorus could be made usable by plants if the rock was treated with sulfuric acid. He called the product "superphosphate," and this term is still used for most phosphate fertilizer.

The phosphate-bearing mineral is called apatite. It is a calcium phosphate, commonly containing fluorine (F); its formula is $(CaF)Ca_4(PO_4)_3$. Apatite occurs in two entirely different forms. The first is a light-green mineral that occurs in some igneous rocks. Rocks with 60 percent or more of apatite are mined in the U.S.S.R. and the Scandinavian countries. About 85 percent of the world's production, however, comes from the other type of apatite, which occurs in sedimentary rocks. The major producers are Morocco and the United States. About 40 percent of the world's total comes from several states in the U.S. By far the largest producer is the state of Florida.

About 2,800 square miles (7254 square kilometers) of flat land in central Florida, east of Tampa, is underlain at shallow depth by a bed of gravelly sediment that is rich in a variety of apatite. This is no place to look for museum-grade specimens, however, as the apatite occurs in sand-size grains and earthy pebbles, which are mixed with clay and ordinary quartz sand. The deposit was laid down in a shallow sea in Miocene and Pliocene time, about 10 million years ago, when the Florida peninsula was covered by water.

The material is worked in open pits by huge excavating machines, called draglines. (One of these is known affectionately by workers as "Super Scooper"; another as "Bigger Digger.") About 20 feet (6.1 meters) of overlying loose sand is removed and dumped into a worked-out section of the pit.

Then the phosphatic gravel is scooped up and deposited in a temporary pit, where hydraulic guns, like super-firehoses, convert it into a watery mixture, or slurry. This slurry is pumped through a pipeline to the washing and concentrating plant, which may be several miles from the mine. There the pebbles and grains of phosphate are separated from the sand and clay. The phosphate then goes to the manufacturing plant, for treatment with sulfuric acid and conversion into superphosphate fertilizer.

This account may make the Florida phosphate operations seem very simple and straightforward. But in reality the industry faces an array of frustrating problems.

Mining phosphate rock in Florida. Big dragline dumps phosphatic gravel into a pit, where high-pressure hoses churn it into a water mixture. This is pumped to the processing plant through pipeline at left.

Consider land. Because the layer of phosphate gravel is thin, flat, and widespread, mining is a land-consuming operation. It cannot be concentrated in a small area. But cattle ranches and orange groves also need land. And Florida—the Sunshine State—has become a center for recreation, tourism, and retirement living, so the mining companies are required to restore the land. There are other land problems, too. A product of the washing plants is a slurry of clay and water, known as "slime." Slime refuses to become solid. After years of standing, it still has the consistency of chocolate pudding. So it must be stored indefinitely, in ponds behind earthen dams. Then there is a waste product from the manufacturing process, an impure gypsum. No use has been found for this "phosphogypsum," which accumulates in great "gyp stacks." Land covered with slime ponds and gyp stacks is useless for anything else.

Reclamation of mined land for residential use, Florida phosphate district.

Or consider water. To produce one ton of washed and concentrated phosphate rock takes 5,000 gallons (18,425 liters) of water. Although most of this is recycled, about 15 percent is lost, chiefly to evaporation. But citrus groves and growing communities also need water. Once considered limitless, water is now a precious commodity in the phosphate district.

How about air? In 1948, nearby farmers began to notice a decline in their crop yields, and cattle started dying of a mysterious epidemic. The culprit turned out to be airborne fluorine, discharged from the phosphate manufacturing plants, so the operators were required to install equipment to remove this fluorine.

As a result of these problems, the Florida phosphate industry has become one of the most regulated industries in the nation. Nevertheless, it continues to produce much-needed fertilizer for the nation's farmers, and for the home gardener as well.

Sulfur

Elemental sulfur is a bright yellow substance with a resinous luster. It melts at a temperature not far above the boiling point of water, and burns with a blue flame, giving off sulfur dioxide (SO_2). Sulfur may occur all by itself, as a mineral. It also combines with several metallic elements, to form a group of minerals called sulfides; the best known of these is iron disulfide (FeS_2), which is pyrite or "fool's gold." Sulfur is also present in gypsum, and in hydrogen sulfide (H_2S), which occurs in some crude oil and natural gas.

Sulfur is an important industrial raw material in itself. It is even more important because it is the parent of sulfuric acid (H_2SO_4). This acid has so many industrial uses that it is known as the "king of chemicals." About 60 percent of the acid is used in making phosphate fertilizer. But sulfur and its acid are also used in petroleum refining, and in making rayon, film, paper, dyes, rubber, and a long list of other products.

If sulfur is so widely used, why do we never see any? And why do we encounter sulfuric acid only in the laboratory of Chemistry 1, where we learn that it burns holes in our skin and clothing? The answer is that sulfur and its acid are used chiefly at intermediate stages of manufacture, somewhere between the raw material and the finished product. Sulfur is combined with other substances in such products as matches and automobile tires. Or it may be discarded somewhere along the line, as in phosphate manufacture; in that process, as we noted, sulfuric acid is used but the sulfur ends up in stacks of waste gypsum.

There was little demand for sulfur until about 1200 A.D. when gunpowder, which contains 10 to 15 percent sulfur, became important in warfare. Demand greatly increased some four hundred years later, when Johann Glauber, a German alchemist, discovered how to make sulfuric acid. The source of sulfur in those days was the island of Sicily, where yellow native sulfur occurs in volcanic deposits. Later, pyrite from ore deposits was "roasted" to separate the sulfur from its

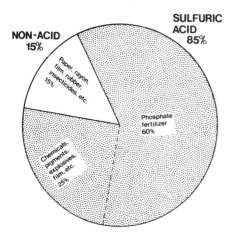

The uses of sulfur. Although this element and its acid go into practically everything we use, their production is most closely related to that of phosphate fertilizer.

companion element, iron. A big breakthrough came in 1895, when a German-born American, Herman Frasch, devised a method of producing sulfur from underground deposits through wells. The Frasch method is based on a simple fact: sulfur melts at 110° C (230° F). Wells are bored to sulfur-bearing rock, and superheated water at high pressure is pumped down. The hot water melts the sulfur, and, since sulfur is nearly twice as heavy as water, it flows downward and accumulates at the bottom of the well. It is then raised to the surface through a pipe inside the water-injection casing. An air lift is provided by compressed air introduced through a still smaller pipe within the sulfur line. The sulfur reaches the surface as a dark liquid, 99.5 percent pure. It is fed into bins, where it cools and hardens to a bright yellow mass; or it may be put directly into insulated barges or tank cars for shipment.

Molten sulfur is deposited in a storage vat, where it will cool and solidify.

A more recent major source of sulfur is the hydrogen sulfide that occurs with much natural gas. Also, environmental requirements now cause sulfur to be recovered from smelters, coal-burning power plants, and general manufacturing processes.

The process of phosphate manufacture is essentially the same one patented by Lawes in 1842, though on a vastly larger scale. Washed and concentrated phosphate rock is treated with sulfuric acid. The sulfate (SO_4) of the acid simply changes places with the phosphate (PO_4) of the raw material:

$$3H_2SO_4 + Ca_3(PO_4)_2 \quad yields \quad 3CaSO_4 + 2H_3PO_4$$

sulfuric	phosphate	anhydrite	phosphoric
acid	rock		acid

In actual operation, the calcium sulfate comes out as gypsum $(CaSO_4 \cdot 2H_2O)$, rather than anhydrite. The phosphoric acid is the desired product: in solid form, superphosphate fertilizer ready to use.

WASHING AND CONCENTRATING PLANT

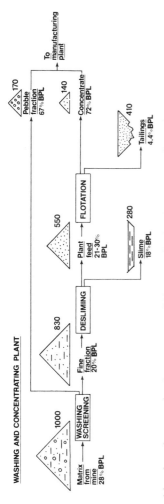

Processing Florida phosphates: what happens to 1,000 tons of mined material. Only 310 tons come out at the right as feed for the manufacturing plant. The remainder is lost as slime and sand. BPL, for "bone phosphate of lime," is a measure of phosphate content.

MANUFACTURING PLANT

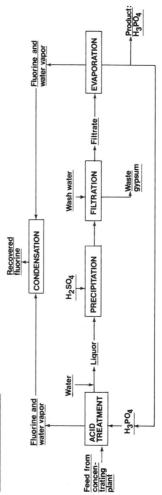

Phosphate concentrates are treated with sulfuric acid for conversion into fertilizer. Fluorine is produced as a by-product, and gypsum as waste.

31

4

Industrial Diamonds: At the Cutting Edge

Most people think of diamonds as precious stones, and indeed they are the most desired of all gems. From engagement rings to crown jewels, the diamond stands alone.

The diamond also stands alone in industry. Here its importance rests on a single property: its hardness. The diamond is the hardest natural substance known. More than 75 percent (by weight) of the diamonds produced are of industrial grade. Industrial diamonds are those that are off-color, flawed, or broken, and are therefore not suitable for use as gems. In addition to these natural stones, synthetic diamonds have been produced since the 1950s and now account for more than half the total by weight. The synthetic product is largely in the form of fine particles, known as "grit."

Diamond is a mineral, one of the two natural forms of the element carbon, the other being the mineral graphite. (The carbon in coal, derived from plant remains, is not a mineral.) If you can remember the third letter of the alphabet, you've got the formula for both diamond and graphite. Two minerals could hardly be less alike. Graphite is soft, black, and slippery; it is the "lead" in lead pencils. The difference lies in the internal structure: graphite is layered, whereas diamond has a rigid three-dimensional framework. Synthetic diamond is made from graphite, but in nature the two minerals are unrelated and occur in entirely different types of deposit.

Diamond grit and powder, mixed with powdered metal or ceramic material, are formed into disks. One form is the diamond wheel, by which other abrasives and hard materials are sharpened and ground to precise measurements. Another is the diamond saw, which cuts metal and stone with ease. In the mining and oil industries, diamond-set bits are used for drilling hard rock. A large diamond may be pierced by a needle-shaped steel drill moistened with olive oil carrying diamond dust; it is then used as a die through which metal is drawn to make wire. The diamond is so hard that the drilled hole will retain its precise size indefinitely. The diamond is

On the desolate coast of southwest Africa, parallel trenches are cut in the beach sands in the search for diamond-bearing gravels.

well adapted for automated cutting and grinding operations, which may be left unattended for long periods. In fact, modern high-speed manufacture may be said to rest ultimately on the cutting edge of the diamond.

Diamonds originate in a rare dark-green igneous rock, named kimberlite from Kimberley, South Africa, a locality famous for its gemstones. Only a small part of today's production of industrial diamonds comes from kimberlite, however. The kimberlite and associated rocks have been deeply eroded by streams. As a result, diamonds and other resistant minerals are found in deposits of stream gravel or, if the streams entered the sea, in beach deposits where ocean currents moved them along the shore. Since diamonds are heavy, they accumulate at the bottom of sand or gravel deposits. Big earthmoving equipment removes many feet of sand to get at these concentrations. To obtain 1 gram (1/28 ounce) of diamonds it

Overburden of dune sands makes trenching for diamonds expensive. It is economical only because most of the diamonds found are of gem grade.

is often necessary to remove 25 tons of sand!

Diamonds are recovered from these alluvial sands and gravels by such simple processes as washing and screening. First the light minerals, mostly quartz and clay, are separated from the heavier fraction. The heavy minerals are then washed across a belt or table coated with grease; the diamonds stick to the grease, whereas the other minerals do not. Another method of separation is electrostatic. Dry diamond-bearing sediment is passed between electrically charged rotors; the diamonds are less conductive than the other minerals and fall separately.

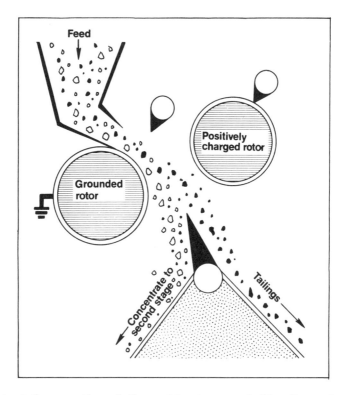

Electrostatic separation of diamond-bearing gravel. The diamonds, less conductive than the other minerals, fall directly downward. One "pass" seldom makes a complete separation, so a series of units is commonly used. "Tailings" are waste.

The United States has no resources of natural diamonds. Most of the production comes from the Republic of Zaire in central Africa, the U.S.S.R., South Africa, and Namibia (South-West Africa). Synthetic diamonds are manufactured in the United States and several other countries.

The standard unit of weight in the diamond is the metric carat, or one-fifth of a gram. Total world production of natural diamond in a recent year was 31,100,000 carats. This seems like a lot, but it equals only 13,712 pounds (6170 kilograms), or less than 7 tons. Prices of industrial diamonds ranged from $4 per carat for small sizes to $65 per carat for stones large enough to be used in wire-drawing dies. This translates into $9,000 to $147,000 *per pound.* So we have been talking about a commodity that is small in bulk but very high in value. Indeed, the industrial diamond is among the most valuable of all the minerals used in industry.

Diamond saw cutting structural concrete. The blade is set with small synthetic diamonds. Water spray is for cooling, lubrication, and dust suppression.

5

Fibers, Films, and Flakes

One mineral occurs in fine fibers that can be made into yarn and cloth. Another goes into products ranging from face powder to house paint. A third lubricates machinery and helps make steel. A fourth gives sparkle to greeting cards and holds the red-hot wires in your toaster. Let's take a look at each of these unique minerals.

Asbestos

A few members of the mineral kingdom are composed of strong, flexible fibers. The name asbestos, meaning "unburnable," was given to these minerals by the ancient Greeks, who used fibers as wicks in their oil lamps. The oil would burn but the wicks would not. Asbestos has come a long way since then. Fibers up to 2 inches (5.1 centimeters) in length can be combined with cotton or rayon and spun into thread and woven into cloth, for such products as fireproof safety clothing and theater curtains. The much more common short-fiber asbestos, with fibers less than 0.5 inch (1.3 centimeters) long, is used in floor tile, asbestos-cement pipe and paneling, paper products, brake linings, and a variety of other products.

Most of the asbestos in use today is the mineral chrysotile, a hydrous magnesium silicate. The most important deposits in the free world are in the province of Quebec, south of Quebec City and northeast of Montreal. Here, in a range of low hills, are masses of a dark green rock called serpentine. Distributed through this rock are innumerable veinlets of chrysotile. Each veinlet is packed solid with silky fibers, which extend crosswise from wall to wall. The veinlets are 3 to 5 feet (0.91 to 1.5 meters) in length and width but seldom more than an inch (2.5 centimeters) thick; they may be compared to very thin pancakes with tapering edges. When broken free, a piece of chrysotile is yellowish green (the name means "golden fiber"), but when broken down into its individual fibers it makes a white fluffy mass like cotton.

The serpentine rock, with its veinlets, is mined in bulk; it is then dried and crushed in a mill. Fortunately, the walls of

Asbestos ore. The desired fibers of chrysotile asbestos are in the light-colored veinlets; all the rest is waste. View is about 2.5 feet (0.76 meter) across.

the veinlets are smooth, so that crushing tends to free the fiber. Passed over vibrating screens, the particles of solid rock make a lower layer and the loose fibers make a layer on top. The fibers are then whisked off the screen by air suction, the way a vacuum cleaner picks up dirt. The fiber goes to the manufacturing plant, the crushed rock to waste piles.

In the past, many persons who spent their days working with asbestos in factories and other industrial sites contracted lung cancer from breathing air laden with asbestos dust. With government encouragement, industries have long since corrected this dust problem; but, as asbestos has been used in many schools and other public buildings, people have naturally become alarmed at a possible health hazard. The asbestos fibers in building materials, however, are tightly held in cement, synthetic resin, or some other binder; they are not free to float in the air and normally pose no hazard to health.

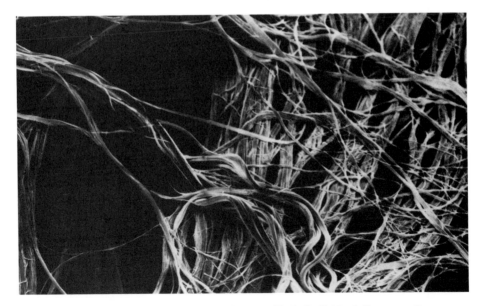

Fibers of chrysotile asbestos, greatly magnified. Individual fibers are finer than a human hair.

Talc

Every mineral has certain properties that set it apart from others. Sulfur, we have seen, is yellow and easily melted; diamond is hard; asbestos is fibrous. The property that distinguishes talc is softness: you can scratch a piece of talc with your fingernail. The mineral is also slippery, so that some varieties are known as soapstone. Pure talc is white, pale tan, or pale green, but no matter what its original color, its powder is brilliant white. It can be ground to extremely fine particle sizes. A silicate of magnesium, talc is inert in most situations, which means that it doesn't react with other substances with which it comes in contact. All these properties make talc a most useful earth material.

When the lady of the house powders her nose, or applies a little soothing talcum powder to the baby, she is using exceptionally pure talc that probably came from a deposit in Montana, Italy, or Australia. Many thousand tons of talc are used every year in cosmetic products.

As you might expect, however, the really big tonnages of talc are used in industry. For example, talc is well adapted for use in paint, where its softness helps make the paint flow smoothly. Because talc is opaque, it has good "hiding power" to cover previous surfaces. In exterior use, it tends to weather to a white powder, and thus is valuable in "self-cleaning" paints.

Another major use of finely ground talc is in ceramics, especially porcelain and other high-grade whiteware. Using talc as a raw material eliminates the development of a network of fine cracks in the product, known as crazing. Because talc has a very low electrical conductivity, it is used in making such ceramic products as switches and insulators.

In plastics, talc reduces the amount of the more expensive organic resins required, and gives strength to the product.

Talc is a competitor of kaolin in the manufacture of fine paper, especially in regions where kaolin deposits are scarce or absent, as in the Scandinavian countries.

Talc is one of those minerals that form deep in the earth, in regions of mountain building. Beds of the magnesium-rich sedimentary rock called dolomite have been converted to talc by metamorphic processes, or by the action of hot silica-bearing fluids coming from bodies of magma. Therefore, deposits of talc are exposed at or near the earth's surface only where great thicknesses of overlying rocks have been stripped away by erosion. In the Inyo Mountains of southeastern California, talc occurs in steeply inclined beds that must be mined underground. Exceptionally pure deposits in the Ruby Range of southwestern Montana are near the surface and are mined in open pits. This Montana talc is of such high quality that it can be economically transported by rail to the West Coast and by

Winter scene in a talc mine in New York. Truck takes crude talc to mill for grinding. Stock pile at left.

ship to Belgium, where it competes with European talcs. Other deposits are found in the Adirondack Mountains of New York, in Vermont, in Texas, and in more than a dozen countries outside the United States. World production of talc approaches 4 million tons per year.

Graphite

The element carbon is the second most abundant element (after oxygen) in the human body. Combined with hydrogen, it forms the hydrocarbons of coal, oil, and gas. Combined with oxygen, it occurs in the air as carbon dioxide, and in such minerals as calcite. And all by itself, carbon forms two highly valuable industrial minerals. One, as we have seen, is the diamond. The other is graphite.

The common pencil illustrates two of the desirable properties of graphite: softness and blackness. (As you probably know, there is no lead in a "lead" pencil.) Soft lead in a pencil is mostly graphite; harder leads contain a mixture of clay.

The mineral graphite has a sheetlike atomic structure, with weak bonds between the layers, so the sheets easily slide past each other and the mineral is slick and slippery. Indeed, one of the major uses of graphite is in lubrication, especially in situations where oil or grease is undesirable, as in textile machinery. Graphite also lubricates machines where high temperatures are encountered, as in rolling mills for steel.

This brings us to another valuable property of graphite: it is unaffected by temperatures as high as 3000° C (5400° F). In comparison, its cousin the diamond burns up at 870° C (1600° F). So graphite is used wherever molten metal must be handled. It is a main constituent of the containers, known as crucibles, in which steel, aluminum, brass, and precious metals are melted. Mixed with sand or clay, it lines the molds into which the molten metal is poured, giving the surface of the molds a smooth finish so the castings can be easily removed after cooling. Graphite is also used in bricks for lining the furnaces in which steel is produced. These metallurgical uses account for about two-thirds of the graphite used in the United States.

Graphite is an excellent conductor of electricity, and so it is used in carbon brushes for electric motors and in dry-cell batteries. It also goes into paint for tanks, bridges, and similar structures.

So-called graphite fibers, used in such products as fishing rods and tennis rackets, are not really graphite; they are carbon filaments manufactured from rayon or other fibrous carbon-bearing raw material. Synthetic graphite, manufactured from a byproduct of petroleum refining, is used chiefly for electrodes in electric-arc furnaces.

Sedimentary rocks that contain plant or animal remains may become deeply buried in the crust, and heated,

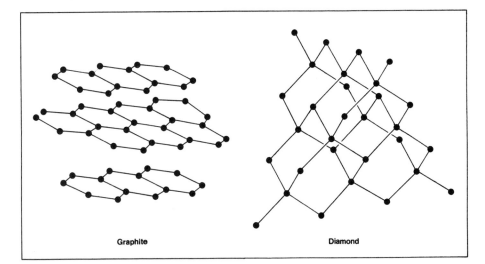

Graphite   Diamond

The two carbon minerals. The carbon atoms in graphite are in sheets, which are weakly bonded and can readily slide over each other. The diamond has a rigid interlocked structure in three dimensions.

squeezed, and sheared by mountain-making forces to form metamorphic rocks. The organic matter is broken down, its hydrogen and oxygen are lost, and the only survivor is carbon in the form of graphite. Thus mineral also occurs in vein deposits and fracture fillings; geologists are not in agreement on how these deposits were formed, except that high pressures and temperatures were involved.

Although the United States is a major user of graphite, it does not produce any. Imports come from Madagascar, Sri Lanka (the island of Ceylon), and Mexico. Other producing countries include China, North Korea, and several European countries. World production totals about 500,000 tons per year.

Mica

It would seem unlikely that any mineral could be in the form of sheets that are thin as paper, clear as glass, and unburnable as asbestos. Yet such a mineral exists. It is a variety of mica, called muscovite or white mica. Big crystals of muscovite are termed "books," since they consist of tightly stacked thin sheets. They occur in a rare form of igneous rock known as pegmatite, where they are intergrown with feldspar and quartz, also in big crystals. Pegmatite is broken up by blasting, and the books of mica are hand-trimmed with hammers to remove other minerals that adhere to them. Clean books are then carefully split, also by hand, into thin sheets several inches across. The sheets are graded by size and transparency. The whole process is costly because of the labor required.

Prehistoric American Indians cut sheets of mica into ornaments. Before heat-resistant glass came into use, mica was used in the doors of stoves and furnaces. Then the mineral was found to have valuable electrical properties, such as low conductivity and the ability to withstand high voltages without rupture. So sheet mica is used in condensers, as a nonconducting element in toasters and other electrical appliances, and in electronics.

The United States produces no sheet mica, mainly because of high labor costs. Most of the material used is imported from India.

Mica in the form of small flaky crystals is a common mineral in many types of rock, and this form of the mineral has a number of uses in industry. Dry grinding yields a white powder for such varied products as joint cement for plasterboard, dusting agent to keep products like roll roofing from sticking together, and material used in oil-well drilling to keep the drilling fluid from leaking into porous rocks. Grinding in water produces a powder of tiny thin platelets with a high luster, which is much used in paint. When the paint is applied, the flakes overlap like shingles on a roof. Wet-ground mica is

Granitic rock in the Spruce Pine district, North Carolina. After crushing and grinding, the rock is processed to yield feldspar, ground mica, and quartz.

also used in printing designs on wallpaper, and it adds the glitter to greeting cards.

The United States is a major producer of ground mica. More than 60 percent of domestic production comes from the state of North Carolina. A major producing district is centered at Spruce Pine, northeast of Asheville in the Blue Ridge Mountains. Production is from a granitic rock that contains about 15 percent muscovite. The rock is mined in bulk and is crushed and ground. The mica is separated from the other minerals—mainly quartz and feldspar—by a process known as froth flotation. The ground-up rock is agitated in water, and a chemical reagent is added that will attach itself to grains of mica but will ignore the quartz and feldspar. The reagent gives a water-repellent coating to the mica grains. The mixture is further stirred up, and a frothing agent, such as pine oil or soap, is added. The mica sticks to the bubbles and rises with them to form a froth, which is skimmed off by paddles or simply overflows. The mica is then washed, dried, ground, and bagged for shipment.

The mining companies are mainly feldspar producers, and sell their mica to other companies that process it for final use. World production of ground mica is about 300,000 tons per year, or more than 40 times as much as that of sheet mica.

6

Four Very Special Minerals

It would not be correct to state that there are only four more minerals that might be discussed in this book. Actually there are at least a dozen. For example, feldspar is an important ceramic raw material; fluorite goes into air-conditioning units and helps make aluminum; garnet is a high-grade abrasive. But we have to stop somewhere. So in this chapter we will discuss two minerals, barite and diatomite, that are unrelated in either geology or use, and two others, rutile and ilmenite, that occur together and are used for the same purpose.

Barite: the heavyweight

If you picked up a chunk of barite—a grayish ordinary-looking nonmetallic mineral—your first reaction would almost certainly be "Wow! It's *heavy*!" That it is. Barite has a specific gravity of 4.2 to 4.5—well over four times as heavy as water and 1.7 times as heavy as granite. Barite is barium sulfate, $BaSO_4$, but its value doesn't rest on its chemical composition but on the property that first caught your attention: its high specific gravity.

More than 90 percent of the barite produced is ground to powder and is used in the oil industry as an additive to drilling fluids. In this use it commonly accompanies bentonite, as discussed in Chapter 2.

In many of the world's oil- and gas-bearing regions—for example, the Gulf Coast of the United States—wells are routinely drilled to depths of 15,000 to 20,000 feet (4,572 to 6,096 meters). At these depths, pockets of gas under very high pressure may be encountered. The drill bit may penetrate a rock with gas under so much pressure that, if uncontrolled, it would blow the drill pipe out of the hole, wreck the rig, and quite possibly catch fire. Such disasters may be avoided by loading the drilling fluid with a weighting agent, making the mud column so heavy that gas pressures are unable to lift it out of the hole. Barite is ideally suited for this purpose. It is not only heavy but also inert and clean, and it mixes readily

Beds of high-quality barite, marked with white stripes, at a deposit in the Shoshone Range, Nevada. Material between the barite beds is flint.

with water and bentonite. Thus it is used worldwide for deep hazardous drilling.

Marine geologists, working from research vessels along the west coast of the United States, have found unexpected evidence as to how some mineral deposits may have formed. On the crests of oceanic ridges, at depths of several hundred feet, plumes of hot mineral-bearing waters gush upward into the cold sea water. The most striking of these, known as "black smokers," are dark with sulfide minerals in turbulent jets at a temperature of at least 350° C (662° F). But there are also "white smokers," which contain mostly silica and barite. All these insoluble materials must come to rest on the sea floor. As it happens, beds of barite in ancient rocks are commonly associated with beds of flint and other silica-rich rocks; so it seems likely that many barite deposits originated from "white smokers" in seas of the past. The largest barite deposits in the United States are in Nevada, where they occur in rocks of Devonian age. Other deposits are found in Arkansas, Missouri, Georgia, and many foreign countries.

Because the use of barite is tied closely to the oil industry, production decreased markedly in the 1980s as oil prices decined and drilling was curtailed. World production in 1981 was over 8 million tons, but a few years later it did not amount to more than half that figure. We may expect it to increase when the oil industry revives.

Diatomite: what diatoms did with silica

In Santa Barbara County, in southern California about 12 miles (19.3 kilometers) inland from the Pacific Ocean, are large deposits of a soft white rock called diatomite. Large quarries are in operation near the town of Lompoc and the Vandenberg space-shuttle center. There are other deposits in Nevada, Oregon, and Washington, but the ones in California are by far the largest.

In Miocene time, about 15 million years ago, the Lompoc region was covered by an arm of the sea. The waters were clear and shallow, and conditions were right for the growth of microscopic marine plants called diatoms. Each diatom consists of a minute speck of protoplasm—a single cell—enclosed within a shell, or "test," of opaline silica (SiO_2 with a variable amount of chemically combined water). Most Miocene diatoms, like those of today, were floaters; when they died, their insoluble tests of silica sank to the bottom and accumulated. The resulting deposit is diatomite.

You can get an idea of the size of these creatures by the fact that a single cubic inch of diatomite may contain 40 million tests. Even more remarkable is the incredibly complex structure and ornamentation of the tests. Some have bilateral symmetry and look like boats, ladders, feathers, and needles; others have radial symmetry and resemble wheels, discs, and golf balls. Enlargement under the electron microscope shows surface details—ridges, spines, holes, dimples—down to dimensions of only 2 or 3 thousandths of a millimeter.

Because of their various and complex shapes, diatom tests don't pack closely together, so the rock is extremely porous; thus it makes an efficient heat insulator. But the most important feature of diatomite is its enormous suface area. If we could iron out all the irregularities of all the tests in a half pound of diatomite, we would obtain an area the size of a football field. No other substance, natural or artificial, has a comparable surface area.

Most diatomite is ground to powder. More than half of the output is used in filtering liquids, including water, wine, beer, syrup, antibiotics, oils, and solvents. A coating of diatomite on the filter cloth presents about 2.5 million capillary openings per square inch; and small amounts of the powder are continuously added to the liquid to be clarified. The fine powder, with its enormous surface area, catches the impurities. Adding new powder builds up a layer that constantly presents a fresh filtering surface.

Used in paint, diatomite has a strong "flatting" effect. The angular diatom particles roughen the surface of the paint film, diffusing the light that strikes it and producing a flat non-glossy finish. Diatomite is also used as a filler in plastics and rubber, as a carrier of insecticides for spraying on crops, and in a variety of other applications.

Much ingenuity is applied to the selective quarrying of diatomite, and to the production of many grades for sophisticated industrial uses. Nevertheless, the value of this versatile material rests on the strange and wonderful things that one-celled plants did with silica some millions of years ago.

Diatomite for filtering, magnified 500 times.

Titanium minerals: a business built on sand

You may be surprised to learn that part of your house is made from beach sand, and not only that but from beach sand that was mined on the other side of the earth. What part of your house—its concrete? glass? bricks? No. Its paint.

We have already mentioned a few minerals used in paint, for example, talc, mica, and diatomite. But these are only additives. The main body of the pigment—which gives the paint its color and also its ability to hide previous coats—is a brilliant white powder, titanium dioxide (TiO_2). Colored paints are made by adding a little intensely colored pigment to a TiO_2-based white paint.

Titanium dioxide is manufactured from either of two minerals: rutile (natural but impure TiO_2) or ilmenite ($FeTiO_3$). United States production of these minerals is small, and we rely heavily on imports. Chances are that the pigment in your

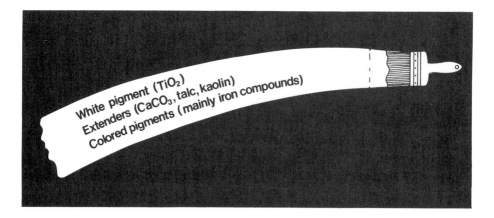

White pigment (TiO_2)
Extenders ($CaCO_3$, talc, kaolin)
Colored pigments (mainly iron compounds)

The chief mineral ingredients of paint. The main pigment is titanium dioxide (TiO_2). Ground calcium carbonate ($CaCO_3$), talc, and kaolin dilute or "extend" the pigment and give special properties. Iron compounds produce mainly red, yellow, and brown colors.

paint come from some 10,000 miles (16,000 kilometers) away—from sand along the beaches of Australia.

You could probably find a few grains of rutile or ilmenite in a bucket of sand from almost any beach. Unlike quartz—the overwhelmingly dominant mineral of such sands—rutile is dark red, and ilmenite is black. Furthermore, both are heavy, with specific gravities above 4 (compared with 2.65 for quartz). Together with magnetite and a few others, rutile and ilmenite are commonly called "heavy minerals."

Mining companies are interested in heavy minerals, but not in a few grains per bucket. They must produce thousands of tons. It turns out that Australia is fringed with hundreds of miles of sandy beaches that contain 5 to 10 percent of titanium-rich heavy minerals. Rutile, the preferred mineral, is abundant on the east coast; ilmenite is found mostly on the coast of Western Australia. Though less desirable than rutile, ilmenite is present in larger quantities and is extensively mined.

There are plenty of sandy beaches a lot closer than Australia; why do we have to go so far for our heavy minerals? The answer is that Australia has stood above sea level for much of geological time, unlike North America, which has been repeatedly submerged and covered by sedimentary rocks. Thus Australia's geologic history has been one of erosion. Great thicknesses of granitic rocks have been weathered and carried away by streams. As is usual under such conditions, feldspar and mica were decomposed to clay and washed to the sea, where they presumably ended up as deposits of marine mud. But quartz and the heavy minerals resisted decomposition, and were liberated from the parent rocks as loose grains. Carried down stream courses to the coasts, and distributed along the shores by waves and currents, they formed the beaches that constitute today's mineral deposits.

How can it be economical to mine a sand deposit that contains only about 5 percent of desirable material? First, the available tonnage is enormous. Second, mining conditions are relatively favorable, and the 95 percent of waste quartz sand can simply be redeposited on the beach. Finally, no hard rock must be crushed or ground up at great expense: nature has already done the crushing and grinding.

After the sand is dug or dredged, the heavy minerals are separated from the quartz by simple techniques based on their different specific gravities. The "heavies" are then passed through magnetic and electrostatic equipment, which separates them into magnetite, ilmenite, and rutile fractions. The two titanium-bearing minerals are then ready for shipment overseas. Rutile goes to one type of pigment-manufacturing plant, ilmenite to another. Complex chemical treatment results in a finished powder of brilliant whiteness. Plants for production of TiO_2 have been built in most of the industrialized countries. World production totals more than 2 million tons per year.

This, then, is how your house happens to be (in a manner of speaking) painted with beach sand from Australia.

apatite—A calcium phosphate mineral, commonly containing fluorine. It is the valuable mineral of commercial phosphate deposits.

artificial brine—Water forced down wells to a salt deposit and pumped back to the surface saturated with salt.

asbestos—A general term for fibrous minerals.

ball clay—High-quality clay suitable for use in ceramics; so called from an early custom of forming the clay into balls for handling and shipment.

barite—An exceptionally heavy nonmetallic mineral, barium sulfate, $BaSO_4$.

bentonite—A clay, formed from the alteration of volcanic ash.

black smoker—A jet of hot water, dark with sulfide minerals, coming from a vent in the sea floor.

book—A large crystal of muscovite mica, in which the sheets are tightly stacked like the pages of a book.

borax—A clear crystalline mineral, hydrous sodium borate, $Na_2B_4O_7 \cdot 10H_2O$.

china clay—Light-colored clay, mostly kaolinite, suitable for making high-quality ceramics.

chrysotile—A fibrous mineral, a hydrous silicate of magnesium. It is the chief form of asbestos used in construction.

colloidal gel—A mixture of extremely small particles of clay in water, such that the clay will not settle but remains in suspension indefinitely.

crucible—A container that will withstand great heat, as in handling molten metal.

diamond—An ultra-hard crystalline mineral, a form of carbon, C.

diatom—A floating microscope single-cell plant that grows in fresh or salt water, often in enormous numbers. It secretes a shell, or test, of silica.

diatomite—A soft porous light-colored rock consisting of the microscopic tests of diatoms.

dragline—An excavating machine that is situated at the upper edge of the pit and digs by pulling a bucket toward itself.

drilling fluid—A mixture of water and bentonite, sometimes with barite or other additives, used in drilling wells for oil or gas.

evaporite—A general term for any mineral or rock that formed as the result of evaporation of a water body.

Frasch method—A technique for obtaining sulfur by pumping superheated water down wells, melting the sulfur, and bringing it to the surface in molten form.

froth flotation—Separating the grains of a given mineral from other minerals in a ground-up rock by stirring up the material in water, introducing a chemical that will attach itself only to grains of the desired mineral, and floating off these grains in a froth formed by adding soap or a similar substance.

granite—A common igneous rock, made up of visible interlocking grains of feldspar, quartz, and minor dark minerals rich in iron and magnesium.

graphite—A soft black slippery mineral, a form of carbon, C.

grit—Synthetic diamond in fine particles.

halite—A clear or white crystalline mineral, sodium chloride, NaCl. It is the mineral of rock salt.

heavy minerals—Dark minerals, such as ilmenite and rutile, that occur in sands and are much heavier than the quartz that makes up most of the sand.

ilmenite—A dark heavy mineral, iron titanium oxide, $FeTiO_3$.

kaolin—A soft white clay, consisting mostly of the mineral kaolinite.

kaolinite—A white clay mineral, a hydrous silicate of aluminum.

kimberlite—A dark-colored igneous rock in which diamonds are found at Kimberley, South Africa, and in similar deposits elsewhere.

metamorphic rock—A rock derived from a preexisting rock by heat, pressure, and chemical changes at depth in the earth's crust.

mica—A group of complex silicate minerals, which split into thin sheets or flakes.

muscovite—A variety of mica that occurs in large crystals in pegmatites and in small flakes in igneous and metamorphic rocks.

NPK fertilizer—A plant food that contains nitrogen, phosphorus, and potassium.

paper clay—Kaolin that is suitable for use as a filler and coating in high-quality paper.

pegmatite—An unusually coarse-grained igneous rock, commonly having the composition of granite.

pelletizing—Forming a powdered material, such as iron ore, into small balls or pellets for ease in handling.

phosphate—A general term for rocks that contain enough phosphorus to be of commercial importance.

phosphogypsum—An impure gypsum, a waste by-product in making phosphate fertilizer.

pigment—Powdered mineral matter that gives paint its color.

potash—A general commercial term for minerals and compounds that contain potassium.

rutile—A dark red heavy mineral, titanium dioxide, TiO_2.

sedimentary rock—Consolidated sand, mud, or shell fragments that accumulated in layers at the bottom of a body of water; also, chemical precipitates such as salt and trona, produced when a water body dries up.

serpentine—A dark green metamorphic rock that may contain veinlets of chrysotile asbestos.

slime—A mixture of water and clay, produced as waste in the processing of Florida phosphate rock.

slurry—A mixture of water and a powdered material, often used for transportation by pipeline.

soapstone—A soft metamorphic rock made mostly of talc.

soda ash—A commercial term for sodium carbonate, Na_2CO_3.

Solvay process—A method of manufacturing soda ash using salt brine and carbon dioxide. It was developed by Ernest and Alfred Solvay.

sulfur—A bright yellow mineral, S, that melts at a low temperature.

superphosphate—Fertilizer manufactured from phosphate rock.

surface area—The total exposed area of an object or material. The surface area of finely divided material is the sum of the surfaces of all the grains.

sylvite—A clear, white, or flesh-pink mineral, potassium chloride, KCl.

talc—A soft, slippery, light-colored mineral, a magnesium silicate.

test—The siliceous shell or covering of diatoms and certain other microscopic forms.

titanium minerals—Ilmenite and rutile.

trona—A clear or white crystalline mineral, hydrous sodium carbonate, $Na_3H(CO_3)_2 \cdot 2H_2O$. It is the source of commercial soda ash.

volcanic ash—Pulverized rock material blown from a volcano in explosive eruption.

white smoker—A jet of hot water, white with precipitated silica and barite, coming from a vent on the sea floor.

Further Reading

Bates, R. L., *Geology of the Industrial Rocks and Minerals,* New York: Dover Publications, 1969.

Bates, R.L., *Stone, Clay, Glass: How Building Materials Are Found and Used,* Hillside, N.J.: Enslow Publishers, 1987.

Bates, R. L., and Jackson, J. A., *Our Modern Stone Age,* Los Altos, Calif.: William Kaufmann, Inc., 1982. Available from American Geological Institute, Alexandria, Va. 22302.

Blakey, A. F., *The Florida Phosphate Industry: A History of the Development and Use of a Vital Mineral,* Cambridge, Mass.: Harvard University Press, 1973.

Ellison, S. P., Jr., *Sulfur in Texas,* Austin: Texas Bureau of Economic Geology, Handbook 2, 1971.

Fuzesy, A., *Potash in Saskatchewan,* Regina, Saskatchewan Geological Survey, Report 181, 1982.

Harben, P. W., and Bates, R. L., *Geology of the Non-metallics,* New York: Metal Bulletin, Inc., 1984.

Multhauf, R. P., *Neptune's Gift: A History of Common Salt,* Baltimore: Johns Hopkins University Press, 1978.

Taylor, G. C., *California's Diatomite Industry,* Sacramento: California Geology, vol. 34, p. 183-192, 1981.

Index

A
anhydrite, 30
apatite, 24
Arkansas, barite in, 51
artificial brine, 8
asbestos, 39-41
Asia Minor, borax in, 13
Australia, 55-56
  talc in, 42

B
ball clay, 18
barite, 49-51
beach sands, 35, 54-56
bentonite, 15-18
bit, 16-17, 34, 50
black smokers, 51
bone meal, 23
Bonneville Salt Flats, 7
books of mica, 46
borax, 5, 13-14
Boron, Calif., borax at, 14

C
calcium carbonate, 54
California
  borax in, 13, 14
  diatomite in, 51
  talc in, 43
Carlsbad, N.M., potash at, 10
China, 18
  graphite in, 46
china clay, 15, 18-19
chrysotile, 40
clay, 15-22
Cleveland, salt mine at, 8
colloidal gel, 16
Cornwall, England, kaolin at, 21
crazing, 42
Cretaceous volcanic ash, 16
crucibles, 44

D
Death Valley, borax in, 13
Devonian
  barite, 51
  salt, 7
  sylvite, 10
diamonds, 33-37, 44, 45
diatomite, 49, 51-53
diatoms, 52
dolomite, 43
draglines, 24
drilling fluid, 17, 47, 50-51
drilling, oil and gas
  barite, use in, 50-51
  bentonite, use in, 16-18
  mica, use in, 47

E
electrostatic separation, 36, 56
England, 18, 21
Eocene
  china clay, 19
  trona, 12
evaporites, 5

F
feldspar, 19, 21, 46, 48, 49, 55
fertilizer
  phosphates, 28-31
  potash, 8-10
filtering, 52
flint, 51
Florida, phosphates in, 24-27
flotation, 48
fluorine, 24, 27, 31
fluorite, 49
Frasch method, 29
froth flotation, 48

G
garnet, 49

63